FLORIDA

GALLERY BOOKS
An Imprint of W. H. Smith Publishers Inc.
112 Madison Avenue
New York City 10016

This edition first published in U.S.
in 1990 by Gallery Books,
an imprint of W.H. Smith Publishers, Inc.
112 Madison Avenue, New York, New York 10016

ISBN 0-8317-8829-1

Printed and bound in Spain

For rights information about the photographs in
this book please contact:

The Image Bank
111 Fifth Avenue, New York, NY 10003

Producer: Solomon M. Skolnick
Author: Jennifer Grambs
Design Concept: Lesley Ehlers
Designer: Ann-Louise Lipman
Editor: Joan E. Ratajack
Production: Valerie Zars
Photo Researcher: Edward Douglas
Assistant Photo Researcher: Robert V. Hale
Editorial Assistant: Carol Raguso

Title page: A lone mangrove stands in the still waters of its marshland home as the sun sets on a typical Florida Everglades sight. Opposite: One of Florida's tallest buildings towers above the St. Johns River in Jacksonville, the nation's largest city. Overleaf: Jacksonville's multi-colored evening skyline hints at the city's bustling, industrial daytime. "The working son in the Florida family of playboys" aptly describes this center of the banking and insurance industries.

A state with something for every one of the nearly 13 million people who live there and the 40 million who visit annually, Florida has Native Americans and cowboys for the more rugged folks, endangered wildlife and exotic fauna for environmentalists, beaches and theme parks for leisure lovers, space shuttles and moon launchings for the high tech minded. And smack in the center of the state beams a large, smiling mouse who is as magic as the kingdom he calls home.

Both the sunny resorts of the Sunshine State and the space age wonders of Cape Canaveral have their roots in Florida's unique past. The low-lying peninsula that forms this tropical paradise owes its origins to fiery volcanoes which were protectively enfolded by water. The land is all part of the Floridian Plateau that even now remains partially submerged less than 50 fathoms beneath the Atlantic Ocean and the Gulf of Mexico. The Plateau has always reacted calmly to any geologic movement, its gentle rolling motion resulting in but a few hilly regions and a downward "dip" into the Gulf of Mexico.

Despite its sea parentage, the Florida peninsula is not, as one might suspect, a gigantic coral reef. Instead, less than one percent is coral. Florida's bedrock, 4,000 feet deep, is cemented with skeletons of

microscopic sea animals. Repeatedly covered and uncovered by the warm, shallow sea, this foundation was a perfect environment for millions of tiny marine animals, protected in life by shells of lime and, in death, sinking to the ocean floor to form massive layers of limestone. Later, fine sand washed down from the Georgia and Alabama mountains and settled on the Floridian Plateau. This sandy layer was, still later, covered by clay.

Not unlike northern tourists today who head for Florida each winter to escape the cold, great masses of animals during the Pleistocene era sought a warm refuge when a great ice sheet began advancing south from the North Pole. Camels, horses, mammoths, huge sloths, and armadillos came south. Later, saber-toothed tigers, wolves, and lions followed. Fossils of strange beasts like three-toed horses and giant pigs have been excavated, and the huge, elephant-like mastodon found its way here from the Old World, probably by way of Asia.

Top to bottom: *The oldest city in the United States, St. Augustine still retains its sixteenth-century Spanish aura. When pirates arrived searching for bounty, the fortress of Castillo de San Marcos was the city's prime defense. The largest building in St. Augustine, this great protector is a reminder of the city's spirited past.* Opposite: *The now-tranquil fort has housed, among others, Spanish soldiers, American revolutionaries, and Confederate and Union troops.*

Henry Flagler built this Venetian Renaissance tribute to his daughter in 1890. Today, the Flagler Memorial Presbyterian Church stands on the northwest corner of Valencia and Sevilla Streets in St. Augustine. Left: The charm of an old city mellowed by time is ever present. Opposite: The Cathedral of St. Augustine, built in the late 1700's, was destroyed by fire nearly a century later. The rebuilt church is the seat of the oldest Catholic parish in the United States.

Plant fossils, plentiful and
predominantly tropical, are
represented by their living
descendants including fifteen
types of palm, breadfruit,
camphor, elm, and persimmon.

Today, much of South
Florida's native plant life grows
nowhere else in the U.S. Florida's
vegetation is generally dis-
tributed among seven habitats—
flatwoods, scrublands, grassy
swamps, savannas, salt
marshes, hammocks or hard-
wood forests, and high pine-
lands. Nature lovers are
continually astonished by the
plenitude of palm trees or the
sudden appearance of a gigantic orchid in the swamps of
southern Florida's Everglades.
Even the plant life most
familiar to us is steeped in
tradition. Rosemary, for example, was transported here by
the English during their
1763–83 occupation. The blue
iris was sacred to the Native
Americans who used its roots
for medicine.

More than 400 species of
birds have been recorded here.
Perhaps the best known is the

THE
DISCOVERER OF
FLORIDA
JUAN PONCE DE LEON

Above left to right: *Manned spacecraft begin their ascents here at the Kennedy Space Center. Towering 525 feet above the center, the Vehicle Assembly Building is one of the world's largest buildings.* Below: *This display of rockets reminds many visitors of Neil A. Armstrong's and Edwin E. Aldrin's 1969 journey to the moon.* Opposite: *"T minus one second" cues spectators that the space shuttle Discovery is about to begin its voyage.*

mockingbird, voted the state bird in 1927 by Florida's schoolchildren. The largest land birds are the bald eagle and turkey buzzard. But the variety seems limitless—from the common blue jay to the nearly extinct roseate spoonbill, just now being rescued from obscurity.

Animals abound, and many endangered species like the alligator are finally being protected. Gone are the days in the 1950's when children visiting Florida would return home holding pet alligators and baby turtles whose infant shells were colorfully painted with palm tree motifs. Turtles today are being protected, especially at places like Jensen Beach on the Atlantic coast, where turtle watches each spring ensure the care of newly-lain eggs.

Aside from the animals and exotic flora, the first explorers who came to Florida encountered a thriving aboriginal civilization. There were perhaps 25,000 people in Florida when Juan Ponce de Leon, probably guided by a map made in 1502 that was the first to show Florida, landed on the East Coast somewhere between St. Augustine and the St. Johns River in the Easter season (in Spanish, *Pascua Florida*) of 1513. The natives were tall, powerful, and enormously hostile to the newcomers—an enmity that would endure until the last 200 survivors were removed to Cuba by the departing Spaniards when Spain ceded Florida to Britain in 1763. Less than 300 years after Columbus discovered the New

Preceding pages: *Space technology at its most spectacular—the ascending space shuttle and its rocket leave a trail of fire and smoke.* This page: *The Sun Bank Center in Orlando soars skyward.* Left: *Orlando's nickname, "The City Beautiful," is reflected in a variety of ways.*

World, Florida's natives had vanished, and the only traces left of them were their burial mounds.

It was the quest for riches—especially gold—that brought de Leon and successive waves of Spanish explorers and conquistadores to Florida. All were looking for material goods when the region's real value lay in the trade routes through the Straits of Florida and the Bahama Channel. Pirates, however, already knew the value of these routes—the key to the Caribbean from the Atlantic. These French, English, and Dutch sailors cruised the coastal waters and the channel, preying on Spanish galleons bringing treasure and goods between the New and Old Worlds.

With British ownership of Florida came a migration from the American colonies. These new settlers included Creek Indians from Georgia, who would become known in Florida as Seminoles.

But rule from London was short-lived. While Britain was distracted by the rebellion in its colonies to the north, the Spanish recaptured Pensacola and western Florida, and in 1783—20 years after acquiring the land—the British crown gave what remained back to Spain. Less than 40 years later, Florida became part of the growing new nation to the north; Spain gave it up to the U.S. in 1821, and 24 years later it became the 27th state.

The nineteenth century brought three wars between whites and Seminoles, as well as the American Civil War, during which secessionist Florida was economically devastated. Reconstruction brought new migrations and development, and with the laying of railroad links to the north and the construction of hotels came tourists.

The railroads saved Florida from the bankruptcy that threatened its survival. No wonder Henry Morrison Flagler and Henry Plant have heroic reputations. Plant's Atlantic Coastline Railroad linked Richmond, Virginia, with Tampa and the luxurious Tampa Bay Hotel. Meanwhile, Flagler's East Coast Railroad, started in 1885, originated in St. Augustine and eventually extended southward to make famous Palm Beach, Miami, and finally, Key West. The railroads, therefore, led to today's Florida where tourism, agriculture, and electronics rank as major industries; citrus, vegetables, and sugarcane dominate agriculture; and fish, timber, and phosphate are important natural resources.

Top to bottom: *What was once a run-down neighborhood in downtown Orlando has been transformed into a bustling metropolis called Church Street Station. The streets may not be paved with gold, but they are restored. The Exchange is filled with vintage shops and restaurants.*

Preceding page: *Europe—in miniature—at Walt Disney World's EPCOT Center. An American version of St. Mark's Square surrounds this replicated bell tower that welcomes visitors to a showcase Italy.* This page: *Snow White and one of her seven dwarfs twirl about the Magic Kingdom.* Below: *The 17-story-high Spaceship Earth in neighboring EPCOT Center beckons visitors to a glimpse of the future.*

But it is the tourists who have put Florida on the map, coming yearly to pack themselves into every nook and cranny of its 8,500-mile tidal coastline.

Before Mickey Mouse and his friends moved here back in 1971, the lure of palm trees and sandy beaches gave Florida its playland reputation. But today Walt Disney World alone, just outside of Orlando in central Florida, attracts millions of visitors each year. The sun shines brightly on this resort, twice the size of Manhattan, which offers re-creations of exotic places, fascinating exhibits and films, and many more sights than could be listed here. Fairy tales seem to come true in Disney's pristine 27,400 acres, which encompass 45 attractions including the Magic Kingdom, the educational EPCOT Center, and the newest addition, Disney-MGM studios, where guests can learn some of the secrets of special effects.

Classic French architecture helped inspire Cinderella's Castle, a masterpiece of fantasy, resplendent with 181-foot-high golden spires. Below: Mickey Mouse's famous face is the subject of this floral portrait. Opposite: Daily carillon recitals ring out over the 128 acres of garden that surround Bok Tower in Lake Wales. 57 bronze bells (the largest weighing in at 11 tons) are nestled inside the marble and stone structure.

Water-skiing performances are a daily routine at Cypress Gardens, which has drawn tourists since the 1940's. Esther Williams filmed her famous underwater scenes here. Below: Cypress trees loom over more than 8,000 varieties of plants and flowers. Opposite: A snowy egret rests on a cypress knob in a quiet corner of Cypress Gardens.

Orlando's Sea World may be one of the few attractions in the country where performers live in the water and come out to show off. Below: Meanwhile, Cypress Gardens, once an untamed swamp, offers the tranquility of a peaceful lagoon surrounded by native and exotic fauna. Opposite: Trained water-skiers go to great aquatic lengths to entertain visitors a Sea World.

50 miles east of Orlando on the Atlantic coast is the Kennedy Space Center, birthplace of America's manned space program and the East Coast launch and landing site for the space shuttle. Its Visitor Center is the starting place for tours that provide glimpses of the mammoth Vehicle Assembly Building, some of the current launch sites, and the Cape Canaveral Air Force Station, where early remnants of the U.S. space program can be seen. Visitors arriving on a launch day may be allowed to watch from a vantage point about five miles from the launchpad. Unless you're an astronaut, that's about as close as you can get to blast-off.

Farther up the Atlantic coast, historic St. Augustine retains its old town flavor, living up to its distinction as the oldest permanent European settlement in the United States. The city architecture owes a great deal to its Spanish origin, and much of it has been restored to its colonial past.

The city prides itself on its oldest store museum, oldest jail, oldest wooden schoolhouse, old Spanish cemetery—everything seems old, if not oldest. The Castillo de San Marcos National Monument is the oldest masonry fort in the U.S. St. Augustine is also the home of the Ponce de Leon Hotel, now a college, built by Flagler in 1889 for railroad travelers.

Skyway Bridge, 15 stories above the water and four miles long, spans Tampa Bay and is part of the city's Sunshine Skyway.

The People's Gasparilla, Tampa's rite of spring, gives all who dare a chance to reenact the city's swashbuckling past. Downtown becomes a spectacle of costumed pirates and buccaneers noisily reliving the bravura of the notorious pirate José Gaspar. **Opposite:** *The tranquil early evening Tampa skyline belies the daytime activity that positions Tampa as the nation's seventh-largest port. On average, 51 million tons of cargo come and go annually.*

Preceding page; clockwise: *Theodore Roosevelt was headquartered at the elegant Tampa Bay Hotel during the Spanish-American War. Tampa's commercial district is graced by palm trees and sculptures. Ybor City's Columbia Restaurant was built in 1905 and is still owned by the original family.* This page: *The turn-of-the-century African motif of Tampa's Busch Gardens gives visitors a glimpse of that faraway continent.* Below: *During football season fans turn out in record numbers to see the Tampa Bay Buccaneers at Tampa Stadium.*

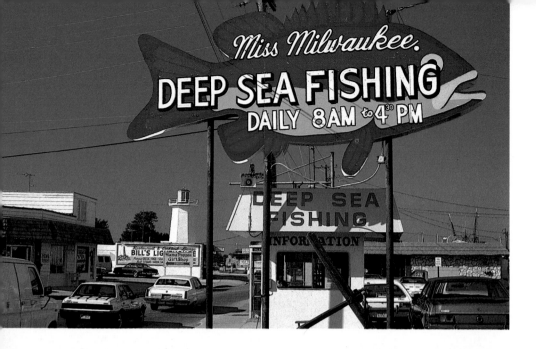

Meanwhile, Jacksonville, near the Georgia border and on the St. Johns River, has the distinction of being the largest city (in land area) in the U.S. while the St. Johns is one of the few rivers to flow northward. The first French Huguenot colony (founded in 1564) is nearby.

Florida has its fair share of lakes—more than 30,000—the largest of which is Okeechobee, 750 square miles of predominantly shallow water. The intrigue of this central Florida territory lies in its western flavor where cattle graze on the open grasslands and cowboys feel at home on the range.

It's possible that no single expanse of open land is as unique as the 1.4 million acres at Florida's southern tip known as Everglades National Park. The name Everglades is a corruption of "River Glades," as an English surveyor dubbed the watery wilderness.

Preceding pages, left: *Spring training camp for the St. Louis Cardinals is in St. Petersburg.* Right: *The Don CeSar Hotel on St. Petersburg Beach has hosted F. Scott and Zelda Fitzgerald, served as an army hospital, and now receives guests in all its restored glory.* Bottom: *MGM's* Bounty *is docked in Miami.* This page, top to bottom: *Sponge docks and deep sea fishing add to Tarpon Springs Greco-American ambience. The Fort Myers home of inventor Thomas Edison. The Belleview Biltmore Hotel, built in 1897 by Henry Plant, claims to be the largest occupied wooden structure in the world.*

Preceding page: *John Ringling must have had his "Greatest Show on Earth" in mind when he built Ca'd'Zan on Sarasota Bay. The mansion, more like a Venetian palace, cost $1.5 million in 1926.* This page: *Naples' Venetian Center, Venetian Bay. The city has come a long way from the mid-1880's when its only access was by water. Below: Some call Naples the Palm Beach of Florida's west coast.*

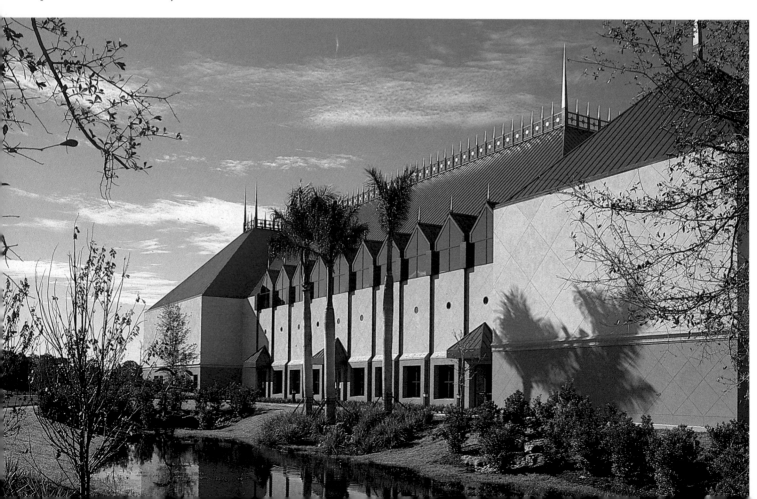

Top left to right: *Henry Morrison Flagler's turn-of-the-century home in Palm Beach is now a museum. Railroad magnate Flagler named the city in honor of the abundant coconut palms he found in the area. The fashionable resort West Palm Beach is the site of a Trump Plaza hotel.* Below: *The Breakers, across from Flagler's former home, is a fitting tribute to the magnate's entrepreneurial skills.*

Pompano Beach, originally a fishing village, is named for a local fish. Below: *The Boca Raton Hotel and Club, designed by Addison Mizner, is a beautiful example of Mediterranean Revival architecture.*

This giant chunk of mysterious nature is actually an enormous, slow-moving river fed by waters from Lake Okeechobee that extends for 200 miles and, in some parts, is up to 70 miles wide. It is home to at least 300 varieties of birds, 600 kinds of fish, and countless other wildlife.

Yet the overall eerie feeling that permeates the Glades probably stems from the multitude of strange-looking plants that grow there. The mangrove for example, sprouts from floating seeds in shallow waters, rising up out of the tide-soaked sand and exposing its twisted roots which collect earth particles and debris. While most of the Everglades is covered by saw grass, cypress trees dot the area and give it an ageless quality. The tree has been called the oldest living thing on the earth and dates back to the Ice Age.

The Everglades took approximately 6 million years to evolve to its present form. Then man came into the picture and the fragile ecosystems that have long taken their natural courses are in jeopardy. Much of what survives in the Glades is threatened with extinction.

Sun worshippers relax under blue skies and swaying palm trees in Miami Beach. Right: *Miami's whitewashed hotels and condominiums reflect a tourist-oriented lifestyle.*

Looking very much like the tiers of a festive wedding cake, this example of Miami's modern architecture rises high above the Atlantic Ocean to the east and Biscayne Bay to the west. Opposite: Miami's impressive skyline is a far cry from what the city looked like a century ago when it was an infant settlement along the banks of the Miami River.

The art deco hotels of the recent past, like this pastel and white example, give Miami Beach its vintage appeal. A quarter of Florida's hotel rooms can be reserved in this small area. Below: Another glimpse of Miami's fabulous hotel architecture.

The Miami Beach City Hall's glass block walls complement the city's prevailing architectural style. Below: *The Miami-Miami Beach Convention Center shows its true colors—pastels.*

However, recent efforts to protect environments like these seem to be making progress, and today the American crocodile and the manatee (sea cow) among others, live safely in these waterways.

If the Everglades is one of the pinnacles of the natural world, then Miami Beach, an island across Biscayne Bay, is a man-made mecca. Not long ago, Miami Beach was America's vacation playground. Today, the resort still attracts a big tourist trade bent on worshiping the sun and taking time out of their hectic northern life-styles to enjoy a leisurely sort of fun.

Miami Beach was simply a sandbar overgrown with swamps and mangroves until Henry Flagler chugged his railroad to Miami in l896, built the Royal Palm Hotel, and watched delightedly as the expected throngs of tourists began to arrive. Meanwhile, Carl Fisher filled in the over-grown sandbar and transformed Miami Beach.

After a period of decline when most families instead visited Disney World, Miami Beach is undergoing a re-juvenation. A stretch of the beach once threatened by erosion underwent extensive

Just east of Biscayne Boulevard the Port of Miami, with its U.S. and Latin American cargo and cruise ships, is one of the busiest ports in the world.

replenishment several years ago, and park areas, once in a state of decline, have been spruced up.

Yet nothing compares with the Miami Beach Art Deco District that incorporates more than 80 blocks and includes 800 buildings. Beginning in the 1930's and 1940's, these hotels have vied with each other for tourists' attention. Pastel colors, flamboyant spires, glass block windows—all these deco devices greeted guests in the resort's early days. Today, many of these buildings are on the National Register of Historic Places.

Continuing down the coast, the southern tip of Florida eases itself along a series of 32 coral and limestone islands linked together by 42 bridges that make up the Overseas Highway. These are the Florida Keys which derive their name from the Spanish word *cayo,* or little island.

The only road that links the keys is this 100-mile-long highway that follows the same path as Flagler's railroad,

This page, top to bottom: *Dolphins, orcas, and sea lions playfully extend their southern hospitality at the Miami Seaquarium. Exotic parrots, macaws, and cockatoos, with all their colorful appeal, welcome visitors to Miami's Parrot Jungle. The Caribbean flamingoes in the jungle's Garden Section offer perhaps the most lingering, graceful memories.*

Vizcaya's sculptured stone barge forms a breakwater in front of the villa.
Below: *Industrialist James Deering's Vizcaya villa is surrounded by formal gardens containing statuary and reflecting pools.*

finished by 1912 and destroyed by the 1935 hurricane. Each key has a quality all its own, so crossing from one key to the next involves a journey to a variety of new environments.

Key Largo, the closest to the mainland, is known as the Diving Capital of the World and boasts North America's only living coral reef. The John Pennekamp Coral Reef State Park was established here in 1960 and protects 78 square miles of reef. It is the first underwater park in the U.S.

Vizcaya's Italian Renaissance-style rooms like this one overflow with treasures. Below: Deering and his designer, Paul Chalfin, traveled throughout Europe to acquire furnishings for the house. Opposite: The Everglades, Florida's only National Park, meanders along the tip of southern Florida and covers more than 1.4 million acres.

Preceding page: *Part of the mystery of the Everglades lies in its maze of lazy marshland that is home to all manner of vegetable and animal life.* This page: *A gator hole where one of the Glades' residents soaks and feeds.* Below: *A great blue heron nibbles catfish from his swampy home.*

The Florida Everglades depends upon a delicate ecosystem for its survival. Opposite: For centuries, the mysteries of the Everglades were shared only among the Seminole who, until 1862, used the swamp-like area as a refuge from the aggressive white man.

The newly-constructed Seven Mile Bridge linking Marathon and Little Duck Key runs alongside its now-defunct predecessor that bears the same name. Both fall a little short of the seven miles their names promise. Below: 42 bridges join all the keys and make up the 113-mile Overseas Highway that extends to Key West. Opposite: Islamorada, the name of the Florida Key that considers itself the sport fishing capital of the world, is Spanish for "Purple Isle."

WHALE
HARBOR
ISLAMORADA, FLA.
CHALLENGER
CAPTAIN DOUG BERRY

Big Pine Key has a forest-like atmosphere and is the home of the tiny key deer, a diminutive, gentle creature that is protected there.

Key West is the southernmost city in the continental United States. Only 90 miles from Cuba, the island has been a refuge for large numbers of Cuban exiles as well as a tourist haven.

Walk through the three-and-one-half-mile-long town, stop in at Ernest Hemingway's house, sip a beer at his favorite bar, and watch the people as they watch you. Take time to look at the sun as it sets, not only on this tiny island, but on all of Florida—its theme parks, Everglades, and amazing beaches—as well.

Preceding page: *The southernmost point of the continental United States is located at the tip of Key West, just 90 miles from Cuba. It boasts, of course, the southernmost house.* This page, top to bottom: *The stunning whiteness of Saint Paul's Episcopal Church attracts worshippers in Key West. The pastel trim on shops and houses along Duval Street adds a Caribbean appeal. Sometimes the spice of a gingerbread motif sums up the Key West spirit.*

This page, clockwise: *The restored Audubon House is named for John James Audubon, even though the naturalist and painter never lived there. Ernest Hemingway actually lived, worked, and most certainly played in this home on the corner of Whitehead and Olivia streets.* For Whom The Bell Tolls, *among other novels, was written in the pool house behind what was once the grandest house on the Key.*

ERNEST HEMINGWAY HOUSE

HAS BEEN DESIGNATED A
REGISTERED NATIONAL
HISTORIC LANDMARK

UNDER THE PROVISIONS OF THE
HISTORIC SITES ACT OF AUGUST 21, 1935
THIS SITE POSSESSES EXCEPTIONAL VALUE
IN COMMEMORATING OR ILLUSTRATING
THE HISTORY OF THE UNITED STATES

U. S. DEPARTMENT OF THE INTERIOR
NATIONAL PARK SERVICE

1968

Preceding page: *This hammerhead shark now makes his home in the heart of the bustling town of Key West.* This page: *The old Strand movie theater still draws attention from photographers.* Below: *Sloppy Joe's Bar attracts crowds of Hemingway fans who, like their hero, like to imbibe.*

This page, clockwise: *Spanish treasure ships really were wrecked off the coast. At the foot of Duval Street, tourists are closer to Cuba than Miami. The sky and the sea continue past Florida's southernmost point.*

Thirty years of building went into Fort Jefferson on Garden Key in the Dry Tortugas, but the bastion was not completed when it was abandoned in 1874. Opposite: In its last decade the fort was a prison. Its most famous inmate was Dr. Samuel Mudd, the physician who set the broken leg of President Lincoln's accused assassin, John Wilkes Booth.

Index of Photography

All photographs courtesy of The Image Bank,
except where indicated *.